Get ready to explc

To get the most c
worth investing in the
the official museum sites in the city – most of which are
covered in this walk. It lasts three days.

https://www.visitbruges.be/musea-brugge-4

Canal Boat Trip

You will probably want to take a canal trip at some point.
There are several departure points which you will pass on
your walk, and several are pointed out en route.   Each
company covers the same route and charges the same amount.
The trip only takes about half an hour. Try to avoid the busiest
times as the boats will probably be packed!

A Potted history

In the ninth century, Bruges was founded as a fortification
against the marauding Vikings who were wreaking havoc
along the northern European coastline. There was a natural
waterway to the North Sea at that time, the river Reie, vital for
transport. In fact the name Bruges is probably from the old
Scandinavian Brygga, which means harbour.

Unfortunately the river Reie had been slowly silting up
since the 11th century, and finally enough silt had been
deposited to seal that vital route to the sea, sending Bruges
into decline. Luckily a new route was dramatically carved out
by a huge storm in 1134. The Zwin channel was created by the
forces of nature, and it stretched to the North Sea from Damme
- a village to the north of Bruges which is still in existence. A
channel was rapidly dug between Bruges and Damme, giving
Bruges vital access to the sea once more.

Bruges was soon a major trade centre.   England and
Scotland were just over the Channel and full of first rate wool,

so canny Bruges traded with both countries and started producing the most luxurious cloths in Europe. Everyone wanted that cloth, so Bruges traded with Normandy for grain, Scandinavia for wood and furs, even spices from the markets of Genoa and Venice. This was the Golden Era.

The Low Countries have always been fought over, and usually belonged to whichever country was the most powerful at the time. With all that trade Bruges started making serious money. France, which was the ruling power in the fourteenth century, demanded more taxes from wealthy Bruges. The town's leaders, the guildsmen, refused to pay. France garrisoned an army in Bruges to collect the taxes, and the guilds reciprocated by murdering anyone in Bruges suspected of being French in just one night – that night was christened Bruges Matins.

The Bruges militia made a judgement on whether someone should live or die, based on whether the unlucky suspect could say a Flemish phrase, "schild en vreind" (shield and friend) without a French accent. The leaders of this revolt were two guildsmen, Pieter De Coninck, head of the weavers, and Jan Breydel, head of the butchers. They are national heroes – you will come across them on the walks.

The French responded to that massacre with an even bigger army, and this time the mighty French Knights rode into battle as well. However they were completely routed by the fast and lethal local militia. It was one of France's worst defeats in history. That battle was named the Battle of the Golden Spurs – because the locals stripped the spurs from the fallen knights and kept them as souvenirs.

The French returned to power just two years later. Despite all this upheaval Bruges grew in power and wealth. Ships from as far as Italy arrived to dock, unload their exotic goods, and load up with the finest cloths.

The city spent its wealth beautifying itself and its people. Life was good and easy until the Zwin, that vital channel to the sea, silted up in the sixteenth century. Without access to the sea, trade plummeted and the wealthy merchants moved out. Antwerp stepped up as the new power in the region, and Bruges went into hibernation for almost four hundred years.

Suddenly at the end of the 19th century, the curious and adventurous rich Europeans rediscovered Bruges. The impetus for this interest was a novel "Bruges la Morte" by Georges Rodenbach, which wakened the world to this medieval city frozen in time, and the tourist trade in Bruges was born.

Bruges has been a tourist city ever since then, although there is once more a commercial link to the North Sea. They built a canal to Zeebrugge on the coast in the twentieth century. The city also does some manufacturing, but mostly it survives on the tourists who can't resist Bruges's charms.

The Maps

There are maps sprinkled all through the walks to help you find your way. If you need to check where you are at any point during a walk, always flip back to find the map you need.

Movie Locations

Not many cities have a major film about them, but Bruges is the exception. The movie "In Bruges" extols the prettiness of the city, and was filmed in many of the places you will be visiting. The movie is about hitmen in Bruges and is worth watching if you don't mind the violence and swearing.

The Walks

There are three walks:

- Walk 1 - Takes you on a loop around the main sights of central Bruges (2.6km).

- Walk 2 - Starts at the Church of Our Lady and takes you out to Minnewater, Bruges's little lake, before returning to the Church (1.8km or 2.4 km).

- Walk 3 - Takes you north of Bruges's main square to explore a less touristy part of town (1.8km).

If you just have one day to explore, use Walk 1 as it covers the most popular sights. If time allows, you can add Walk 2 to it.

Walk 1 – Central Bruges

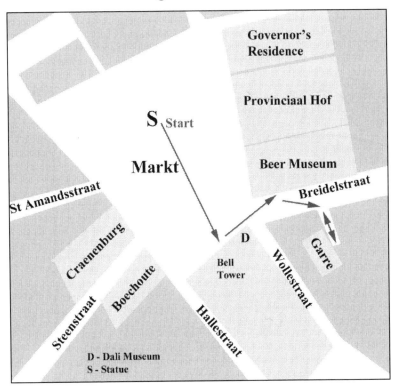

Start this walk by standing in the middle of Markt, the commercial hub of medieval Bruges. It's hard to imagine now, but it was only in 1996 that cars were banned from parking here. Wander over to the statue of local heroes Coninck and Breydel in the middle of the square and have a look around.

This square has been used as a marketplace for over a thousand years, and if you are here on a Wednesday morning you can meander round the fruit and veg stalls.

The statue beside you commemorates the two local heroes. On the pedestal you will see four friezes. If you stand face to face with Coninck and Breydel, the frieze you are looking at depicts the Battle of the Golden Spurs, and if you go to the left hand side you will see Bruges Matins – both of which you read about in the Potted History.

Provinciaal Hof

Now face the bell tower and turn left. The very ornate grey building is the Provinciaal Hof. At one time the West Flanders council sat here, but it's mostly used for ceremonial events nowadays. It looks very gothic but it's actually a bit of a phoney as it was built in 1887, so it's not nearly as old as it looks.

Before the Provinciaal Hof was built, the site was filled by the Waterhalle, a covered warehouse where merchants' canal boats would pull up and unload their goods straight into Bruges's markets. The hall was so vast that it filled the entire side of the square. Sadly it fell into total disrepair long ago and was demolished. The canals used by the merchants are still there but they're underground now.

Governor's Residence

To the left of the Provinciaal Hof you will see a darker grey building with a single high turret. This was the Governor's Residence although no Governor actually ever stayed there. When it was built, the diggers found some of the pillars from the long gone Waterhalle. They are now in the Arentshof garden which you will see later.

Recently the Governor's House was restored and is now the Historium museum – a "multimedia experience" which involves walking from room to room and watching a love story set in medieval times. Whether you want to visit depends on how much time you have to visit the real Bruges.

Now turn towards the Bell Tower which dominates the square.

Bell Tower

It went up in 1220 and it has been added to, and rebuilt several times over the centuries. It was even higher at one point with a wooden spire, but that was destroyed in a fire and never replaced.

Longfellow wrote an affectionate poem about it, called the "The Belfry of Bruges". It tells us:

In the market-place of Bruges
stands the belfry old and brown
Thrice consumed and thrice rebuilded,
still it watches o'er the town.

C. K. Chesterton, who wrote the Father Brown stories, was perhaps less impressed by it:

"I have been standing where everybody has stood, opposite the great Belfry Tower of Bruges, and thinking, as everyone has thought (though not, perhaps, said), that it is built in defiance of all decencies of architecture. It is made in deliberate disproportion to achieve the one startling effect of height. It is a church on stilts. But this sort of sublime deformity is characteristic of the whole fancy and energy of these Flemish cities...

...All Gothic buildings are full of extravagant things in detail; but this is an extravagant thing in design. All Christian temples worth talking about have gargoyles; but Bruges Belfry is a gargoyle. It is an unnaturally long-necked animal, like a giraffe. The same impression of exaggeration is forced on the mind at every corner of a Flemish town. And if anyone asks, "Why did the people of these flat countries instinctively raise these riotous and towering monuments?" the only answer one can give is, "Because they were the people of these flat countries." If anyone asks, "Why the men of Bruges sacrificed architecture and everything to the sense of dizzy and divine heights?" we can only answer, "Because Nature gave them no encouragement to do so."

The Tower originally held the town archives and treasury, but after a fire both offices were moved into the Burg, which you will see later. The tower has been both a bell-tower and a watchtower over the centuries. It also leans, in fact the top leans as much as a metre off the centre.

Although the building which the tower rises up from looks a bit like a church, it's not. It was actually the cloth hall where Bruges stored and traded its goods. In 1399 there were 384 merchant stands in the halls.

Above the Markt entrance you can see the balcony where the town officials would stand to proclaim the "Hall Commandments" – the rules and regulations about trade and industry.

It is a bit of a climb up with 366 steps, but it's worth it. There are a few side rooms on the climb up, so you can stop to catch your breath without causing a traffic jam.

Go through the gate beneath the balcony. Pause for a moment to imagine all those market stalls of long ago in the halls on your left and right, and then use the stairs at the side of the courtyard to reach the ticket office on the first floor. Before you go up the tower, have a look at the balcony in the ticket office that the many official proclamations were made from. Then start climbing!

The first room is definitely worth a look. The treasury is a brick vaulted room with gated chambers holding the treasure chests. Those huge chests held the precious official documents of the city, and were locked with ten keys. Eight of the keys were held by the various guilds, and the final two by the Mayor and a senior member of the clergy. It needed all ten of them to open the chests, so it must have taken quite a bit of organisation!

The second room explains how a carillon works, because the bell tower is actually a carillon – no need for campanologists here! The principal is the same as a simple music box, a drum plucks the tune out, and the only difference is scale.

The third room shows you the hour bell, Maria, which weighs in at six tons and is a replacement for an even heavier bell which cracked centuries ago.

The fourth room lets you see the carillon in action. The huge drum you see picks the tunes out by tugging the bells in the right sequence. It is the largest brass drum in the world. There are four tunes played in an hour and the drum is reset every two years to a new set of tunes. The current set of tunes is listed on one of the columns in this room. The bells ring out every fifteen minutes, so you don't have to wait too long to see and hear them in action.

Finally you will reach the last level which is where the bells are. You can see the ropes which are attached to each bell and are tugged by the drum below.

You might want to wait the fifteen minutes to hear the bells at close quarters. While you wait you can get some good views out of the windows. Make sure you don't miss the windows to the left of the doorway as you entered, where you can see the huge canal to the north of the city which goes all the way up to Zeebrugge.

When your ears stop ringing descend very carefully to the ground.

The Bell Tower starred in several key scenes in the film "In Bruges". My particular favourite was when Ray tried to dissuade a rather chubby tourist from attempting the climb, warning him that the climb would kill him. You might feel he wasn't exaggerating.

Dali Museum

Back on ground level, there is an art gallery in the right cloth hall which holds some of Dali's paintings and sculptures. It's quite eye-catching in dali-esque pink. It's worth a look if you like modern art and you are a Dali fan.

Return to the Markt and Coninck and Breydel. Face the Bell Tower again and turn right.

Craenenburg café

On the corner of Sint-Amandsstraat, you will find the Craenenburg café with its slim corner turret.

It's worth noting this guild house, because this is where Archduke Maximilian of Austria and his advisor Lanckhals were held captive by Bruges when he tried to impose higher taxes in the fifteenth century. Maximilian was part of the Hapsburg family which ruled huge parts of Europe for centuries. He took control of Bruges and Flanders when his wife Maria of Burgundy died in a horse-riding accident.

His advisor, poor old Lanckhals, was tortured and executed by Bruges and Maximilian was forced to watch his end. Maximilian eventually escaped, and when he later became Emperor of the Hapsburg Empire he got his revenge:

Firstly he diverted vital trade to Antwerp, and secondly he instigated a new law: Bruges had to keep swans on its canals "until the end of time". This sounds a strange law, but it was because swans have long necks, or Lanckhals, just like his departed advisor. As you explore you will see the swans gliding around the canals, so give a thought to Lanckhals when you see them.

Boechoute

On the other corner of Sint-Amandsstraatt is Boechoute, the oldest guild house on the square. The top of this building is quite complicated. If you look up, you will see a gleaming globe and a weather vane on the roof. On the front of the

14

building is what seems to be a compass. The compass is actually connected to the weather vane and shows which direction the wind is blowing in.

The globe is even more intriguing. It's part of a device which helped in the days when timekeeping was not an exact science. Frequently the cities of northern Europe were on different times which caused great confusion when trying to run a railway. When the sun shines and hits the globe it casts a shadow onto the square. Walk towards the corner of Sint Amandsstraatt to see the line of copper stamps running into the square, each one marking where the sun hits the line on a particular day, giving us the local meridian line. Not much use on a cloudy day of course.

Guild Houses

Round the other two sides of the Markt you can see many more guild houses, now housing cafes and restaurants. They each have a wall decoration which symbolises the guild which once resided there. The guild houses have been extensively rebuilt, and they do make a pretty sight.

Before you leave the Markt, try to imagine the boats pulling up to the Waterhalle, the merchants buying and selling in the cloth hall, and the guild members going in and out of the guild houses, all busy making money.

Now stand facing the bell tower. Turn left to go into Breidelstraat, and at number 3 on your left you will find the Beer Museum.

Beer Museum

This museum has been installed in the old post office, and if you are a real beer fan you will want to visit. Belgium probably has more varieties of beer than any other country, and it is an intrinsic part of the culture.

You can buy a ticket with or without an included beer tasting. You will be given an iPad to guide you around the exhibits, and at the end of the tour you can then taste some of the product – if you opted to buy that ticket. You might want to visit the museum after you have explored Bruges!

Continue along Breidelstraat which will eventually take you into Bruges's second square, Burg. However before you get there, keep your eyes on the right hand side of the street for a very narrow opening, known as Garre – it's very easy to miss.

Staminee De Garre

Follow this little alley and climb the steps to find the well-hidden little bar, Staminee De Garre, which dates from the eighteenth century with old oak beams and wooden tables.

If you don't feel like a beer right then, it's well worth returning later in the day to sample their beer and enjoy the atmosphere. Their speciality is Tripel De Garre. Warning: it's 11%. If like me you don't like the taste of beer, try the peach beer which is quite different and very refreshing.

Note – If you visit in the evening, you will know when it's closing time, as they always finish with Ravel's Bolero.

Return along the little street to Briedelstraat.

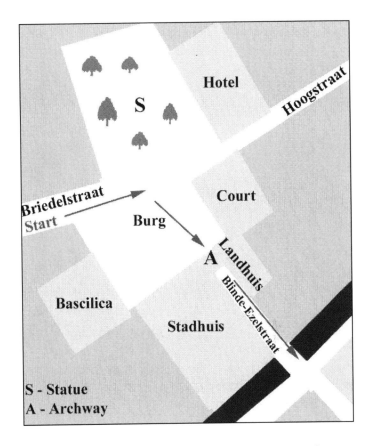

Briedelstraat
Start

Burg

Hotel

Hoogstraat

Court

Landhuis

Blinde-Ezelstraat

A

Bascilica

Stadhuis

S - Statue
A - Archway

Turn right into Breidelstraat once more. As you do you can have a look in the windows of the various lace shops lining the street, and gasp at the prices! However making hand-made lace is an incredibly skilled and time-consuming task so perhaps those prices are justified.

Burg

If the Markt was the commercial centre, this was the rather more ornate administrative centre. Originally it is where Bruges castle stood, but sadly it has not survived. However as you enter the square you will see the beautiful Stadhuis (Town

Hall) on your right, with its stunning windows, and colourful façade.

Stadhuis

The Town Hall is really old; it was built in the fourteenth century and has governed Bruges ever since. Inside is one of Bruges's not-to-be-missed sights.

Outside, the façade is decorated with many statues, starring Adam and Eve, various biblical characters, and Flemish leaders. Sadly many of the originals, which were brightly painted by Van Eyck, were smashed by the French in the eighteenth century. The niches on the façade lay empty for centuries and it wasn't until relatively recently that one of Bruges's most loved mayors championed their replacement. So the statues you see today are quite modern but they are so skilfully made you think they are the originals. When you go inside you will be given a little guide to the cast of statues on the facade. Remember to keep it safe until you come back outside.

Beneath the windows are the coats of arms of the surrounding towns and villages which were governed by Bruges.

Go in and climb the large staircase and go through the iron gate to enter the Gothic Hall. It has a stunning oak vaulted ceiling sitting above the colourful walls which are decorated with scenes of Bruges's past. Pick up one of the information sheets at the door which will explain what each of the murals represents. You can pick out various key scenes in the history of Bruges which you will read about as you explore the city. Find the following as they are key points

- The Battle of the Golden Spurs
- The founding of the Order of the Golden Fleece
- The arrival of Christ's blood

Do pop into the museum in the room to the left as it has some old Bruges posters which are interesting. There is also an extremely odd painting at the door - a group of men and one of them is wearing what looks like very painful body jewellery. Perhaps you can figure it out.

When you exit, turn around to face the Stadhuis again. You can now use your little guide to identify the various statues.

On the bottom row you will see a knight among the biblical characters. This is Baldwin Iron Arm who eloped with Judith, the daughter of French King Charles the Bold. Charles was not pleased, so the couple fled to Rome to plead with the Pope. The Pope gave them his blessing so the King had to accept his new son-in-law, but he got his own back by sending them away from court to Northern Flanders, i.e. Bruges.

Make sure you go round the corner to the left, just before the archway. Spot Adam and Eve on the top tier of statues. The guide will point out that they are being a bit naughty, or perhaps Adam is just being modest?

19

Face the Town Hall once more and this time turn to the right to see the Basilica of the Holy Blood, decorated with golden statues of knights and angels.

Saint Basil the Great

The Basilica sits above another much older chapel which is dedicated to Saint Basil the Great, and which is more atmospheric than the busier Basilica. Saint Basil's is entered directly from the square, the entrance is to your left and is marked Basilica.

The chapel holds some of the Saint's bones. Saint Basil was a bishop in what is now Turkey. He was very learned but also cared greatly for the poor and disadvantaged, and he gave most of his wealth away to that cause. In Greece St Basil's day is on the 1st of January and is full of family traditions. Just like Santa Claus, Saint Basil gives gifts to the children.

Basilica of the Holy Blood

Return outside and go up the stairs to enter the Basilica of the Holy Blood. Climb the impressive stairway to reach the bright and highly decorated church, with its wonderful wooden roof, colourful walls, and stained glass windows.

This church holds another relic brought back to Bruges in the Second Crusade. The crusades were basically invasions of the Middle East by armies of Christian knights, who thought it their duty to liberate the holy land and return it to Christian hands.

Legend says that one of the knights, Thierry of Alsace, brought back a crystal phial holding a piece of cloth stained with the blood of Christ. The story tells us that Joseph of Arimathea kept the cloth after washing Christ's body after the crucifixion. In fact, no-one knows for sure when the phial arrived in Bruges or who brought it. If you visited the Gothic Hall in the Stadhuis, you will have seen a mural of its arrival in Bruges.

It is kept in a fittingly magnificent chapel with a silver altar on one side of the church. The shrine contains 30 kilograms of gold and silver and more than 100 precious stones. The phial is only brought out of the church on Ascension Day, when Bruges hosts the Procession of the Holy Blood, a grand parade which commemorates national heroes Jan Breydel and Pieter de Coninck. The procession re-enacts the arrival of the phial into Bruges along with various biblical scenes, and is a major event in Bruges's calendar.

https://www.youtube.com/watch?v=YNEIM-eyCdE

The phial is also on show to the public inside the Basilica during the month of May.

Before you go, have a look at the intriguing pulpit which is a globe inscribed with the words "Region Australis Incognita" at the bottom. It looks modern but actually dates from 1728, and was inspired by the Book of Mark which contains the line:

Go into all the world and preach the gospel

The Basilica of the Holy Blood was supposedly visited by Ray and Ken in the film "In Bruges". However, filming was not allowed in such a holy place, so they had to use a quite different church in its place.

Landhuis van het Brugse Vrije

Once you are back outside, the building directly opposite you is the court house. Walk over to stand in front of it and the building on your right is another very attractive building - the Landhuis van het Brugse Vrije or the seat of the Liberty of Bruges. The Liberty is an old term for both Bruges and the surrounding land, and this building was an administrative building.

Before you go inside have a look at the outside where there is a colourful Coat of Arms of Bruges just to the left of the archway. It depicts the bear of Bruges, which according to legend was the first creature seen by Baldwin Iron Arm, the first count of Flanders, when he visited Bruges in the ninth century. Baldwin fought and killed the bear, and then declared the bear to be the symbol of Bruges.

High above you on the right-hand side you can see a golden Aaron; he was the brother of Moses and battled verbally with the Egyptian Pharaoh to gain freedom for his people. In the middle stands Justice, with the lion of Flanders on one side and the bear of Bruges on the other. Finally on the left-hand side is Moses, with one of the tablets brought down from Mount Sinai.

Spot the iron rings beneath the windows. They were used to chain convicted criminals to the wall as part of their punishment, and to make sure the general public saw what happened to wrongdoers.

Now go inside. There is just one room to visit, but it's worth a look. The council chamber has been restored and has a huge fireplace with an impressive oak chimneypiece. Above the fireplace stands a young and almost life-size Charles V, carved in dark oak and marble. There is also a large painting on display showing the council sitting in the chamber, all looking very stern and judgmental at a criminal brought before them.

Saint Donatian

Go back outside and walk straight ahead to the end of the Court building.

Ahead and to your right is a modern hotel. An important cathedral, Saint Donation, was built across this side of the square in 950 AD and housed yet more saintly relics. However it was destroyed by the French in 1799 in the aftermath of the French Revolution, and was never rebuilt.

When the modern hotel was built the diggers stumbled on the Cathedral's cellars and foundations. The hotel construction was allowed to proceed but on condition that what was left of the Cathedral was preserved and that the public had access. The hotel is happy for visitors to look around the cellar unless there is an event going on down there. Just ask at reception and they will point you to the stairway.

Since the hotel sometimes hosts receptions in the cellar the floor is lined with rather out-of-place carpeting and you might find stacks of chars, all of which you should just try to ignore. You will find the old walls and archways of the Cathedral which are worth seeing. There is also a display of various plates and other items which were found during the excavation. Sadly you won't find the tomb of Van Eyck. He was buried in the Cathedral but his tomb has never been found.

Les Amoureuses (The Lovers)

Opposite the hotel and standing among the trees is The Lovers, a rather romantic piece of art representing all the young couples who get married in the Town Hall. You can see "love" written in many languages. It was sculpted by Stefaan Depuydt and Livia Canestraro, the same skilful artists who replaced the missing statues on the Town Hall facade.

Look closely at the pedestal the Lovers are standing on and you will spot a bronze frog. Of course there is a legend.

It's said that if a visitor kisses the frog, he or she will return to Bruges again - so have a go!

Ezelpoort

Stand facing the Stadhuis once more. On the left side you will see an archway called Ezelpoort or Donkey Gate. This was part of the old ramparts which ran around a much smaller Bruges in the thirteenth century. Only the bottom brickwork is the original as it was modified later as Bruges expanded beyond the old city wall.

Go through the archway to reach Blinde-Ezelstraat, or Blind Donkey Street.

Blind Donkey Street

There are various stories on how the street and the archway got its name. One tells of an old tavern which stood here long ago called The Blind Donkey. It supposedly got its name from the blindfold placed on a donkey which had to pull a treadmill all day. Poor creature!

Turn around before you reach the canal to see the pretty archway behind you, with the golden statues of Solomon in the middle, Prosperity to the left and Peace on the right.

Once you are on the canal bridge, look to the left to see the oldest bridge in Bruges, the Meestraat bridge

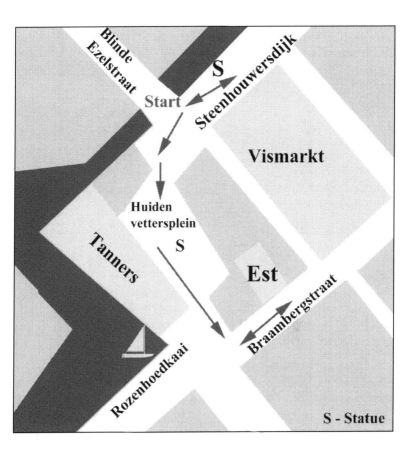

Blinde Ezelstraat

Start

Steenhouwersdijk

S

Vismarkt

Huiden vettersplein

S

Tanners

Est

Braambergstraat

Rozenhoedkaai

S - Statue

Vismarkt

Once over the canal, straight ahead of you is the cobbled Fish Market with its columned arcades. It's still in use, although sadly there are not many fishmongers using it nowadays. At the weekend it turns into an arts and crafts market. So you may see the fishmongers at work and the fish displayed on the stone slabs, depending on which day you visit. Both the Meestraat Bridge and the fish market were used in a romantic scene in the film "In Bruges".

On the right hand side of the market you will see a restaurant renowned for its fish, De Visscherie, and on the balcony above the door is an amusing statue of a fisherman catching a big fish.

Back at the canal side is a bust of Frank van Acker, the first socialist mayor of Bruges, who was so popular he stayed in power from 1976 until his death in 1992. He was the mayor who pushed for the statues on the Town Hall to be restored.

Face Blind Donkey Street, and then turn left to walk into Huidenvettersplein.

Huidenvettersplein

The large building on the right hand side was the Tanner's guildhall in the fourteenth century and there are various bas reliefs on the walls depicting the men at work. However by the fifteenth century their neighbours could no longer stand the smell of tanning leather so they were ousted to a less busy part of town.

The post in the middle of the square with the two lions on top used to have a partner, and together they were used to weigh the hides brought to the tanners. The lions are holding the tanner's guild coat of arms, although it's very worn now.

This is a pretty little square nowadays lined with restaurants and chocolate shops, which is ironic as after the tanners left, it became a second fish market, but it was where the less wealthy came to buy cheaper freshwater fish as opposed to expensive seawater fish.

Leave this little square by the exit opposite the one you entered by and you will be back by the canal side. On your right is a set of stairs to one of the canal boat departure points.

Relais Bourgondisch Cruyce

Before you move on from this corner, look over the canal and to the right. Spot the Relais Bourgondisch Cruyce hotel with its half-timbered façade. That is the hotel the two hit men holidaying "In Bruges" stayed in.

The Corn Carriers House

Once past the steps turn left away from the canal onto Braambergstraat. At number 7 on your left you will see an old building which at the time of writing houses the Est wine bar. Cross the road to see it properly.

The building itself is the house of the Corn Carriers, who loaded and transported grain bags. The Grain Carriers bought the building from the Tanners round the corner when it was a ruin and restored it. You can see two bas reliefs on the outside showing the men at work.

Return to the canal and just beyond is one of the prettiest spots in town.

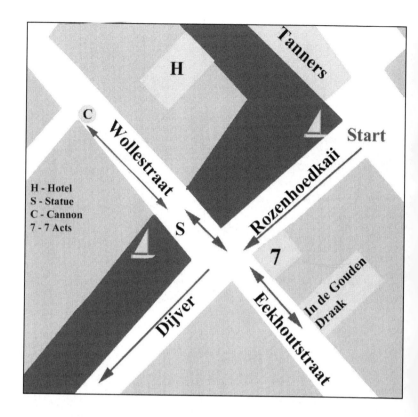

Rozenhoedkaai

This is probably the most photographed spot in Bruges. You should return again in the evening to watch the sun go down. When the lights go on, it's golden.

The salt market was situated here, and is more important than it sounds. In medieval times, salt was precious as it seasoned and preserved food. It's where our word salary comes from, probably because the Roman Legionnaires were paid in salt.

The Seven Works of Mercy

Continue along the canal side and just before you reach the next bridge, stand back and have a look at the building on your left hand side. At the top you will just be able to make out seven bas reliefs of the Seven Works of Mercy, identified in the Bible as the good deeds we should all be trying to do.

- Feed the hungry
- Shelter the homeless
- Bury the dead
- Clothe the naked
- Relieve the thirsty
- Heal the sick
- Visit the imprisoned

John of Nepomuk

Continue along the canal side. When you reach the next bridge, pause for a moment at the statue of John of Nepomuk, standing in the middle of the bridge.

He is the national saint of the Czech Republic, even though he was thrown into the Vltava River in Prague and drowned on the order of King Wenceslas. He was the court priest and his crime was a refusal to reveal the Queen's confession to the King. He is also the patron saint of bridges so he is standing in a very appropriate location.

The battle that never was

Cross the bridge into Wollestraat. Stop when you reach Kartuizerinnenstraat, the first street on your left. Spot the little cannon embedded into the pavement.

In 1631 the Dutch army arrived in Damme, a nearby village and planned to invade Bruges. However the Spanish army arrived to defend Bruges since Spain ruled Flanders at the time. The Dutch army was much smaller than the Spanish army so they decided discretion was the best option and high-tailed it back to Holland. The Spanish army were happy with that outcome and also departed. Bruges heaved a huge sigh of relief, and later found this little cannon where the Dutch army had camped. They placed it here to commemorate the battle which never happened.

The cannon stands at the corner of number 28 and if you look up at its façade you can see a set of bas-reliefs also commemorating the event It's quite an ornate façade and right at the top are more bas- reliefs, this time of Greek Gods Orion, Poseidon and Ceres

Backtrack across the bridge and walk straight into Eekhoutstraat. Just a few houses along you will find number 5 on the left.

In de Gouden Draak

Stand back to see its golden dragon at the top and if you look above the door you will see a very old inscription:

In de Gouden Draecke

It commemorates a black day in the history of Bruges. In the fourteenth century nearby Ghent rebelled against Count Louis II of Flanders mostly over taxes. The Count blocked road access to Ghent to subdue the rebels, and planned to attack from Bruges.

Ghent decided to take the offensive in order to regain access to the sea via the Ghent-Ostend canal which flowed through Bruges. The Ghent army camped outside Bruges, and unfortunately the Bruges soldiers indulged in a lot of beer-drinking and decided to attack when they were too drunk to hit anything. They were decimated by an immediate onslaught by Ghent and the result was that Bruges was occupied by Ghent - although Count Louis II managed to scarper away before he was caught.

If you have ever visited Ghent you will have seen the Golden Dragon which sits at the top of Ghent's bell tower. Legend says it was taken from the St Donation cathedral in Bruges as plunder, and the golden dragon on top of this house commemorates its loss.

Eekhoutstraat

If you were to walk another block to reach Willamstraatt, you would be standing where the oldest sign of man in Bruges has been found, dated from 2000 BC. Sadly though there is nothing to see or to mark the event. So instead backtrack to the canal-side and turn left into Dijver.

There is another boat departure point just past the bridge on the other side of the canal.

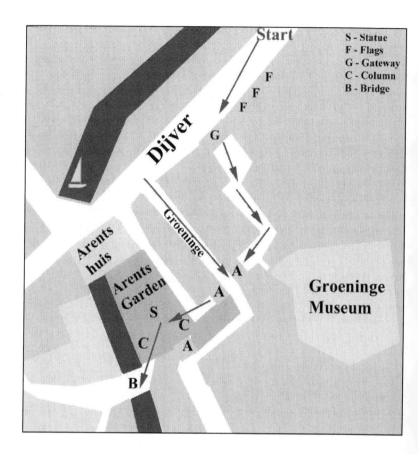

You will pass a building on your left-hand side which is usually lined with flags. Just beyond it is the gateway to the Groeninge Museum. Even if you don't plan to visit the museum, stick with this route as it takes you to a very pretty little bridge.

Note, if the gateway is locked the museum is probably closed, but you can take the next little lane called Groeninge instead to continue the walk from the Arents Garden on page 42.

Groeninge museum

Follow the signs through the garden, and eventually you will reach the museum entrance.

This is Bruges's premier art gallery and has many items worth seeing. The museum has a collection of what are called "Flemish Primitives" which is an odd phrase. It is not a term of derision, but an appreciation of the artists' deep spiritual output. Bruges was the epicentre of this artistic style and the museum houses a priceless collection.

The "Flemish Primitives" collection covers paintings from the 15th and 16th centuries. They are mostly very religious and they stand out by having highly detailed and colourful backgrounds. The key artists were:

- Jan Van Eyck
- Rogier van der Weyden
- Petrus Christus
- Dieric Bouts
- Hugo van der Goes
- Hans Memling
- Gerard David

Note, there are often school-trips to the museum, and if you happen to arrive at the same time as a group, do the museum in reverse. Your museum map shows you the layout of the galleries which are in chronological order, so rather than going into gallery one, turn left and go into gallery 10. You could argue it's a better route anyway, because many people think that art tends to get better and more interesting as you go back in time.

Here are some of the more eye-catching paintings:

The Judgment of Cambyses and The Flaying of Sisamnes - Gerard David

If you like the blood and gore of the old days you might find "The Judgment of Cambyses" and "The Flaying of Sisamnes" interesting.

"The Judgment of Cambyses" shows Sisamnes, a judge under King Cambyses of Persia being accused of corruption. You can see a balcony in the background which shows Sisamnes taking a bribe, and in the foreground a bearded King Cambyses numbers his crimes.

The next painting, "The Flaying of Sisamnes", shows his gruesome punishment. He is flayed alive and four men are busily taking his skin off. I actually think the victim would be showing a lot more horror and pain than the painting portrays.

These two paintings were commissioned to hang in the town hall as a warning to the magistrates of Bruges on the consequences of corruption.

The Last Judgement - Hieronymus Bosch

It's another frightening sight, showing those not good enough to make it to heaven being punished in various horrible ways. Monsters are devouring the sinners and there are even some nuns being boiled alive! It's a very unusual painting given its age – full of little people in a landscape of enormous household items.

The Last Judgement is discussed in depth by Ray and Ken in the movie "In Bruges".

Madonna with Canon George Van der Paele – Van Eyck

Local boy Van Eyck is well represented. This work shows the Madonna and Jesus, surrounded by the kneeling canon, St George, and Saint Donatian – the same saint whose cathedral is now under the Crown Plaza hotel.

St. Luke Drawing the Virgin – Weyden

The original was painted in 1435 and is now in Boston. It was so popular that it was copied over and over again, and this version was painted in the fifteenth century.

Annunciation - Petrus Christus

It's thought that Petrus Christus was an apprentice of Van Eyck. He later moved to wealthy Bruges to continue his career. The Bruges painter's guild had very strict rules, which meant before he could join the guild he had to purchase citizenship. He then became one of the city's leading artists.

This paining shows us Mary being given the startling news of her pregnancy by the archangel Gabriel. It has been beautifully restored and at the bottom you can see that it's signed and dated.

It is thought to be the first painting in Bruges where the artist has used central perspective – which means that figures and items decrease in size as they are painted further into the background, coming to a central point in the distance.

Serenite - Delvaux

There are also more modern works; find Serenite by the Belgian artist Delvaux, who is well known for his depictions of nude women in fantastical settings.

It gives us a good example of central perspective.

The Last Supper – Woestyne

This is a striking large modern painting. There is no clue as to which of the apostles gathered for supper is Judas, but perhaps it is the one Jesus is looking at.

There also seems to be a distinct lack of bread and wine for thirteen of them, and I am sure there was no water into wine miracle on the agenda.

The Three Women at the Tomb - George Minne

This bronze statue shows three women standing with bowed and covered heads mourning at the tomb of Jesus. I think it has a mysterious feeling, and perhaps a little spooky.

There is a lot of argument over who the three women are. The bible mentions three Marys but as you know there were a lot of Marys in the bible – so no-one really knows.

Galileo and Urban VIII - Edmond van Hoven

This painting shows Galileo pointing at the stars, and it looks like he is trying to convince Pope Urban VIII of his theories.

Pope Urban was actually interested in Galileo's theories initially. Galileo made a fatal mistake though when he published his book "Dialogue Concerning the Two Chief World Systems". Pope Urban had asked that the Church's position be put into the book, but unfortunately Galileo complied by inserting a conversation between scientists and a character called Simplico, who maintained the argument that the Earth was the centre of the universe and was portrayed as an idiot.

Not surprisingly the Pope responded by banning it and sent it to the Inquisition for examination for heresy. Galileo was found guilty and was heading for the flames, but he took the wise course of recanting his theories and instead spent the rest of his life imprisoned in his own home. Meanwhile of course, his book was smuggled and read all over Europe.

Louis de Gruuthuse - Unknown

Louis de Gruuthuse was one of the most prominent and richest citizens of Bruges. He was a soldier, diplomat and advisor to Philip the Good, the Duke of Burgundy who ruled Flanders. You will see his palatial family home later in the walk.

If you have visited Ghent you will have read about the Battle of Gavere, which was fought between wealthy Ghent and Philip the Good over taxes. The battle was a disaster for Ghent, losing most of its army and a large numbers of its citizens. It was Gruuthuse who asked the Duke to spare the city from total devastation. The Duke replied:

If I would destroy this city,
who is going to build me one like it?

So Ghent was spared to fight another day.

Portrait of Margaret van Eyck – van Eyck

This was one of Van Eyck's last paintings. It's thought he painted his wife Margaret as a gift, perhaps for her birthday. She is dressed very elegantly in a red robe with a fur collar – probably squirrel. This painting was only discovered at the end of the 18th century when it was put up for sale in a fish market! It was rescued and restored by the National Gallery in London.

When you leave the museum turn left to exit the garden through an archway, cross Groeninge, and go through another archway to reach the Arents Garden.

Arents Garden

This little garden is decorated with a modern sculpture called Riders of the Apocalypse. According to the book of

Revelations the riders were Pestilence, War, Famine, and Death, each riding a white, red, black, or green horse. Oddly there is nothing to indicate which rider is which in this rendition.

There are two columns flanking the main path; these are the remains of the Waterhalle mentioned earlier in the walk when you were in the Markt. They were found when the Governor's House was built.

Arents Museum

If you stand between the columns with the Riders on your right, the Arents museum is the white building diagonally on your left. If you decide to visit you will find the ground floor is for temporary exhibitions, but the upper floors have a permanent exhibition of works by artist Frank Brangwyn. He was born in Bruges to a Welsh father and an English mother.

He seems to have been able to turn his hand to anything; he produced murals, paintings, wood engravings, and even designed carpets, ceramics and stained glass. He did a series of British Empire panels which hang in Swansea.

Bonifaciusbrug

To continue stand between the columns with the horsemen to your left and in front of you is another archway – but don't go through it. Instead, slightly to the right is another little path which will take you out of the Arents Garden.

You will reach another canal and the humped St Bonifaciusbrug. This must be the prettiest bridge in town, although it's not as old as it looks as it was only built in 1920. However it's still a lovely sight. Local legend tells us that any single person who crosses the bridge will marry the first person they see on the other side – so time it well.

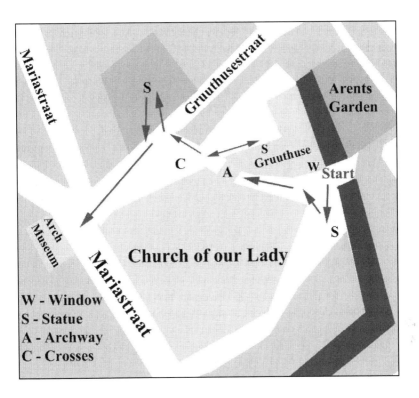

Cross the bridge and once you are over look to your right. You will see the back of the Gruuthuse Museum – spot the tiniest little window on the second floor right next to the canal. Some say it's the smallest window in Europe.

Look along the canal in the other direction for a pretty view of an old timbered house. There is also a statue of Juan Luis Vives beside the canal on your left.

Juan Luis Vives

Vives was actually Spanish, which you might have guessed from the name. His family were originally Jewish but converted to Christianity to stay alive. However most of his family were executed as Judaizeres by the dreaded Spanish

Inquisition – basically they were accused of not really believing in Christ. His father was burned at the stake.

Vives's mother survived that tragedy but then died of the plague when Juan was just fifteen. She was accused of the same crime twenty years after her death – and the Spanish Inquisition was so obsessed that her remains were exhumed and burned at the stake.

Vives abandoned Spain when his mother died and headed to Bruges to start a new life. He was a great scholar and through his work and writings earned the title "Father of modern psychology". He died in Bruges and was buried in the original St Donatian's Cathedral.

The very large church in front of you is The Church of Our Lady which is covered in detail on Walk 2. The church steeple is the second tallest brick tower in the world, beaten only by the tower of Saint Martin in Landshut, Germany.

At the little fork ahead of you, take the right hand path and walk between the church and the Museum through an archway. That archway was put in place so that the lords and ladies of the Gruuthuse family did not have to venture outside to attend church – clearly a very influential family.

Walk through the garden; it is strangely decorated with iron crosses on the left hand side. Those crosses were taken down from churches during World War II and never restored.

Gruuthuse

To the right you can see the courtyard of the Gruuthuse, which was the family home of one of the richest families in Bruges – they more or less had a monopoly on the brewing industry, and were consequently loaded.

If you go into the courtyard you can see the most famous member of the family, Louis de Gruuthuse. He can be seen on a horse above the front façade of the palace. You might have seen his portrait if you visited the Groeninge museum.

Nowadays the building is a museum and it houses all sorts of items, lace, paintings, tapestries and furniture, so it is probably of limited interest to most people – the French extracted the best items long ago. However you can also enter the prayer chapel which is joined to the church and you will get a great view of the tombs of Mary of Burgundy and Charles the Good which are in the Church.

Return to the path; ahead of you across the road lies a little park. Here you will find a statue to Guido Gazelle surrounded by benches where you can rest a little.

Guido Gazelle

Guido was a local priest who was intensely patriotic. He saw the Flemish people as quite distinct from the Dutch. He was also a poet and writer, and he translated Longfellow's Song of Hiawatha into Flemish, mainly because he was very interested in American Indians.

The tower of The Church of our Lady reaches high above you. Face the church and turn right to reach a crossroads. You will see the archaeological museum in front of you. You now have a choice.

If you are have enough time, you could now move to Walk 2 which covers Bruges South. It starts and ends at the church entrance, so once completed you could then finish Walk 1. If that appeals, then turn left at the junction into Mariastraat to find the church entrance and continue from Walk 2 on page 56.

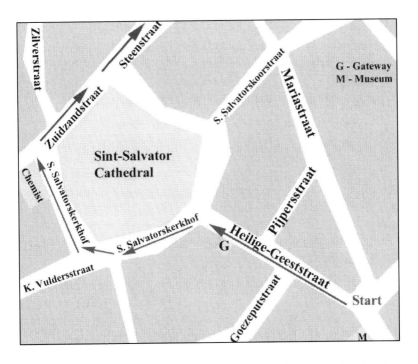

Otherwise continue Walk 1 by turning right at the Archaeological Museum into Heilige-Geeststraat – Holy Ghost Street.

Heillige Geeststraat

You will see the Sint-Salvator Cathedral before you, but before you reach it you will pass an interesting gateway on your left. Behind it is the Bishop's Palace which is not open to the public, but you can admire the monumental gateway with its angels.

Continue and you will reach the Sint-Salvator Cathedral. When you reach it turn left into Sint Salvatorskerkhof and follow it around the Cathedral.

Den Cleynen Thems

When you reach the corner of Zuidandstraat and Sint-Salvatorskerkhof take a look at the chemist on your left. Den Cleynen Thems is the oldest working pharmacy in Bruges, first mentioned in 1484. It's easy to spot as the name is on the side of the building as you approach it.

Walk down the steps to the entrance of the cathedral.

Sint-Salvator Cathedral

The original church only became a cathedral after Belgium finally achieved independence from the French in 1830. It was second choice after the much more central St Donatian, but the French had already destroyed that one in the 18th century. Sint Salvator was not so grand then, so a lot of work was done on it to cathedralize it.

Go in and have a look at the beautiful wall tapestries above the choir stalls. They were woven way back in 1730 originally for St Donatian Cathedral, but were saved when it was destroyed and then restored in the new cathedral.

Below the tapestries you can see a long line of Coats of Arms. They belong to the knights who were made part of the Order of the Golden Fleece. That order came into being in Bruges by order of Philip the Good, the Duke of Burgundy who ruled over Flanders at the time. His idea was to create a body of principled and respected men who would look after and make judgements on the running of large parts of the Kingdom. The Order of the Golden Fleece was a great success and it still survives in part today - there is an order of Knights in Spain and Austria and most of the Kings and Queens of Europe are members of one or the other.

The cathedral also has a museum, and if you visit you will see another famous collection of Flemish Primitives. The most famous piece is the "Martyrdom of the Holy Hippolytus" by Dieric Bouts and Hugo van der Goes.

Martyrdom of the Holy Hippolytus - Dieric Bouts and Hugo van der Goes

This is another rather gruesome scene. Hippolytus it seems was a Roman soldier who found Christianity, and as usual the Roman commander took exception to this and had him killed in a particularly gruesome manner. His four limbs were tied to four horses which were then driven in four different directions, essentially tearing him apart.

Leave the church and turn right passing Zilverstraat on your left. You will see the Bell Tower on Markt in the distance. Leave the square by walking onto Steenstraat.

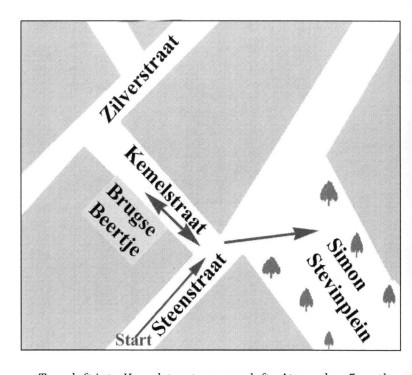

Turn left into Kemelstraat on your left. At number 5 on the left hand side you will find a beer institution, 't Brugse Beertje.

't Brugse Beertje

This is usually a very busy touristy bar, but if you can squeeze in comfortably you can try out one of the many bottled beers available. They have over three hundred brands in stock, and the staff are expert on the beers and the glasses they should be poured into. If it looks too busy or if you don't feel like a beer you can always come back later.

Now backtrack to Steenstraat and turn left. A few more steps will take you into a tree filled square on your right, Simon Stevinplein

Simon Stevinplein

This little square was where the slaughterhouse stood. However in the early nineteenth century, new laws on hygiene sounded its death knell. It was demolished and this square was built to take its place. Bruges decided to honour Simon Stevin by naming the new square after him. He was a renowned scientist and mathematician who came from Bruges.

A bronze statue was ordered for the opening ceremony in 1846. Unfortunately it wasn't ready in time, so a plaster sculpture was painted a bronze colour and used instead. As you might guess plaster statues don't really stand up to North European weather very well, and after a few days of bad weather the bronze paint started to come off. So every couple of nights a new plaster statue was put on the square and the old one disposed of. They kept doing this until September 1847 when the real statue was ready and could finally be installed.

Stevin also has a large crater on the moon and an asteroid in the asteroid belt named after him.

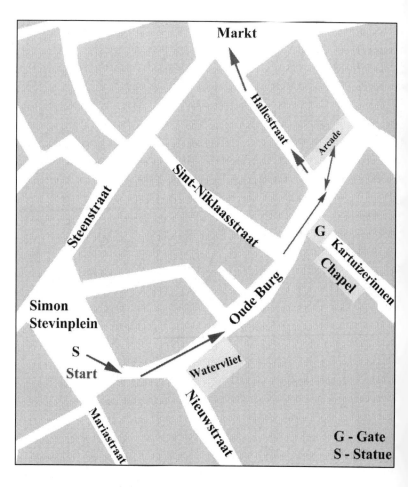

Stand back-to-back with Simon and cross the square diagonally left to walk into Oude Burg. Pass Nieuwstraat on your right and reach a large building called Hof van Watervliet on your right.

Hof van Watervliet

This fifteenth century mansion was built by a local politician but it got its name in the sixteenth century when

54

Marcus Laurin, the lord of Watervliet lived there and gathered together a collection of art, coins and books.

Perhaps more interestingly, the famous English politician Thomas More stayed there when in Bruges. He wrote Utopia, a book about the type of country and civilisation he wanted England to become. He wasn't successful of course as he was beheaded by order of Henry VIII, because he would not recognise Henry as the head of the Church of England, or the annulment of his marriage with Catherine of Aragon. There is a little bronze plaque commemorating his stay at the side of the wooden gate.

Continue along Oude Burg and you will reach a large gateway on the right which leads into Kartuizerinnenstraat

Pro Patria and the Military Chapel

The archway was built in 1929 to honour the dead of World War one. It's topped with the Lion of Flanders.

Go through the gate, the building on your right is the Military Chapel. It was original a monastery but was taken over by the military in the late nineteenth century. Along the wall you will see some plaques commemorating the people of Bruges who died in both WWI and WWII. If it's open do go in. You will find the poignant tomb of the Unknown Soldier.

Now backtrack to Oude Burge and turn right once more. Pass Hallestraat on your left to see an arcade which runs along the back of the Cloth Hall. If you haven't had a browse around any lace shops yet you get another chance here.

Return to the start of the arcade and turn right into Hallestraat, which will take you back to Markt and the end of this walk.

Walk 2 - Bruges South

This walk starts at Onze-Lieve-Vrouwekerk, The Church of Our lady which stands on Mariastraat. If you have already done Walk 1 you will have seen its tower soaring above you.

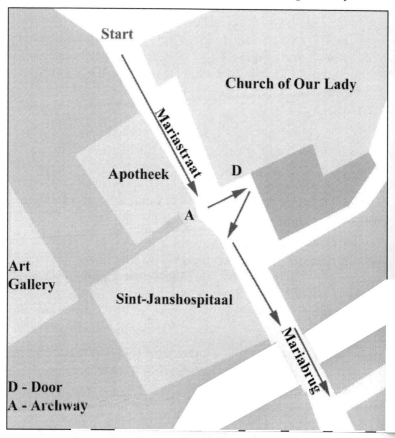

The Church of Our Lady

Make your way to the church entrance which faces a little square just off Mariastraat. Inside you must see Michelangelo's Madonna and Child.

Madonna and Child - Michelangelo

This is the only one of his works to leave Italy while he was still alive. It was bought by a rich cloth merchant from Bruges. It has been snatched twice by invading armies, once by Napoleon and again by the Nazis, but is now safely home.

If you are facing the altar you will find it on the right hand side. It is in a black marble alcove, flanked by red veined columns. To keep it safe from the kind of madman who attacked the Pieta in Rome, it is now behind bullet-proof glass, so you cannot really see it at its best. However you can see that the Madonna looks very thoughtful and sad as she clasps the baby Jesus. It featured in the movie "The Monuments Men", which tells the story of the works of art stolen by the retreating Nazi army.

Wander round the choir which is full of paintings and woodcarvings, but the highlight of the church are the tombs of Mary of Burgundy and her farther Charles the Bold which are in pole position at the front of the altar.

Charles the Bold was the Duke of Burgundy and at that time Burgundy ruled large areas of The Netherlands, which at the time included Bruges. He died in France in battle and his body was brought back to Bruges to be buried. His tomb is next to his daughter Mary's. Her tomb is made of black marble.

Mary of Burgundy was the only child of Charles, well educated, loved to ride and hunt, and was the most eligible heiress in Europe when her father was killed. The King of France longed to regain control over the wealthy Netherlands and insisted that she marry his son who was just a child. At the same time Mary had to reconcile the nobles in her Flemish lands who wanted no interference from France in any of their affairs. She solved all her problems by signing "The Great Privilege", which basically returned control of taxes and government to the Flemish cities, and in return her nobles gave her much needed support and an army to refuse the King of France's demands.

Having got rid of one unwanted suitor, she chose to marry the young handsome Prince Maximillian of Austria instead – he was part of the mighty Hapsburg family. It was a happy marriage, tragically cut short by her death. She died at the age of 25 in a terrible riding accident – her horse threw her, landed on top of her, and broke her back. Her death was a disaster for Flanders.

After she died her husband became regent, but the Netherlands did not want Hapsburg rule any more than they wanted French rule. There were a number of revolts and revolutions, especially when Maximillian hiked the taxes that Flemish cities must pay. At one point Maximillian was imprisoned in Bruges and only the arrival of the Hapsburg army got him out. Eventually the mighty Hapsburg Empire took full control of Flanders and Maximillian got not only his taxes, but took sweet revenge on the cities which had defied him, including Bruges.

The Transfiguration of Christ - Gerard David

The church is also home to an altarpiece decorated with "The Transfiguration of Christ" by Gerard David, one of the artists you read about in the Groeninge Museum renowned for their Flemish Primitives.

The Transfiguration was the moment that Jesus told his disciples who he was, and to prove it his robe turned white, a bright light surrounded him, and he had a chat with the prophets Moses and Elijah - which was a bit of a shock to Peter, James, and John.   You can see their reaction here.

When you are ready to move on, turn left along Mariastraat. You will pass what looks like a church on your right-hand side as you do, but save it for later on the walk. Instead cross the canal by the Mariabrug. Note if you haven't taken the boat trip around Bruges yet, there is another boat trip site just below the bridge.

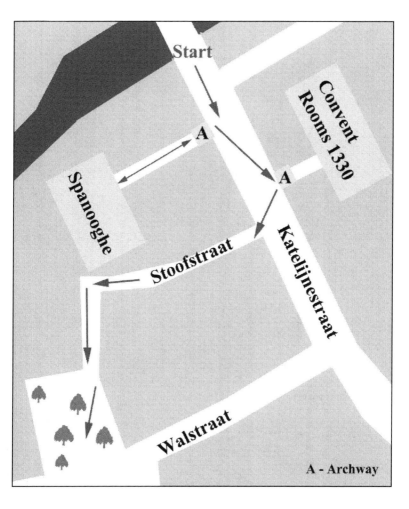

Continue along Katelijnestraat and on your right you will see an archway with "Godshuis Spanoghe" above it.

Spanooghe

The archway takes you into a sanctuary for elderly unmarried women, founded by Francesca Spanooghe in the seventeenth century. Today, the little white alms-houses sprinkled around Bruges still house the elderly and people in need.

Return to Katelijnestraat and turn right. After a few steps you will see another archway on your left with "Rooms Convent 1330" above it.

Rooms Convent 1330

Go through to see another set of little almshouses. It was originally a convent as the name tells you but was converted into almshouses in the fifteenth century.

Return to Katelijnestraat once more and turn left. Another few steps will take you to a little lane on your right called Stoofstraat – it's just after number 28.

Stoofstraat

Stoof means "stove" in Flemish, and this is where you would have come for a hot bath in the middle ages. It was also the medieval red light district. Nowadays it is just a quiet little lane.

Follow it and it will take you around the back of the almshouses of Spanooghe, and into a little square filled with trees.

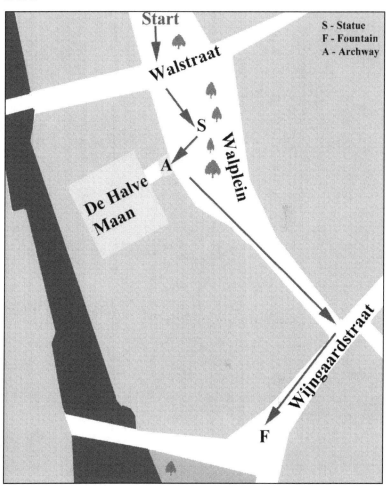

Walk over the square, cross Waalstratt into Walplien, another little square.

Walplien

In the middle of this little square is a crazy modern statue, named "Zeus, Leda, Prometheus and Pegasus Visit Bruges".

Pegasus is clearly the horse; Leda is the naked lady being seduced by Zeus who is disguised as a swan – from a famous Greek legend. That leaves Prometheus as the bowler hatted driver!

Prometheus is also a Greek hero, who stole fire from the gods and gave it to man. He was punished by being bound to a rock and every day an eagle arrived to eat his liver which regrew every night! So it's a mystery why he is portrayed as a coach driver!

De Halve Maan

On the right hand side of the square at number 26 is an archway which will take you into De Halve Maan, the only family brewery still in existence in Bruges and worth a visit. It's really more of a museum than a working brewery. They still do some brewing but most of the actual production takes place in an out of town modern facility.

They brew a beer called "Brugse Zot" on the premises. The name comes from a tale about the unpopular Maximilian of Austria's visit to Bruges. After entertaining the visiting Emperor with a parade of jesters and fools, the leaders of Bruges petitioned Maximilian for permission to have a yearly fair to finance a madhouse. Maximilian was obviously not impressed with Bruges, and replied "Bruges is already a madhouse". I guess he had not forgiven them for imprisoning him and killing his advisor. That name stuck and the citizens of Bruges are nicknamed Brugse Zotten - the fools of Bruges.

You can purchase a guided tour including a beer tasting, however you should check if an English tour is scheduled. You will climb up and down the brewery, including a visit to the roof of the building where you will get a good view of the ground you have covered. Finally you will be taken to the beer-house and given a sample of their product. The tour lasts about 45 minutes.

Wijngaardstraat

Leave the brewery and turn right to leave Walplein. Next, turn right into Wijngaardstraat - this little street is mostly full of cafes these days. You will reach Wijngaardplein.

Horsehead Fountain

Wijngaardplein is a lovely green spot with a rather odd fountain – it hosts two horseheads and the fountain water gushes from the horse's mouths. This is where the horse-drawn carriages stop for a rest. There are lots of little cafes around here if refreshments are needed.

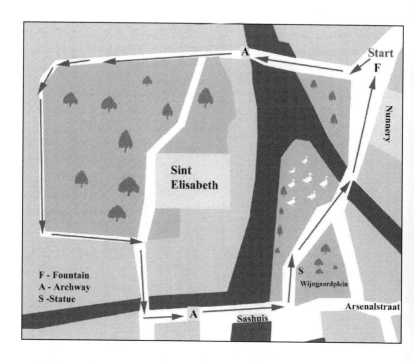

Turn right to cross the bridge. Go through the archway with 1776 in large golden figures above it to enter the Begijnhof, but have a look at the statue of Saint Elizabeth of Hungary adorning the gate as you do. The church you will soon see is dedicated to her. She is holding a basket to represent the food and help she gave to those in need. Beneath the gate is also written the word "Sauvegarde'" which means Safeguard.

Begijnhof

This tranquil oasis is where the beguines lived. The Begijnhof was founded by Countess Margaretha of Flanders to help devout women who were left with no family or income after the wars took their menfolk away, but who could still care for themselves from making lace etc.

The residents wore habits and prayed but were not actually nuns - they were free to leave the Begijnhof and visitors could enter during the day. Only at night were the gates locked.

The Begijnhof was started in the thirteenth century although the houses have been rebuilt over the years - the oldest surviving house is from the fifteenth century. There are no more beguines today; the Begijnhof is now looked after by Benedictine nuns.

Walk around the green lawn. If you visit in spring you will find the lawn awash with gaily coloured daffodils waving in the spring breeze. The pretty scene was painted by Winston Churchill.

You can visit the little church and museum. The church is dedicated to Saint Elizabeth of Hungary.

Follow the path around the lawn and you will see a lane with white cottages on either side leading away from the lawn. Follow this lane and turn left to go through an archway. You will find yourself at the edge of the Minnewater

Minnewater

This is the lake of love and there is a romantic legend associated with it.

Minna was a beautiful maiden whose father arranged her wedding to Horneck. However Minna loved Stromberg. When the Romans invaded, Stromberg went into battle, but pledged his love to Minna. Minna begged her father to let her marry Stromberg, but he refused and the marriage to Horneck was arranged. The night before the wedding she fled to the forest and did not return.

Stromberg returned, searched the forest, and found her hidden on the bank of a stream. But he was too late and she died in his arms. Stromberg dammed the river, buried Minna in the river bed, and let the water flow again covering her grave. The lake took its name from Minna's grave. Legend also says that if you cross over the lake bridge with your partner you will have eternal love!

Back in the real world this lake was built with a purpose; the water entering it feeds Bruges's canals.

Sashuis

The building you see on the right-hand side of the bridge is the fifteenth century Sashuis (lock-house) which regulates the water level of the canals running through Bruges from the lake behind it. It makes a nice snap. It's said to be lucky to throw some coins over your shoulder into the water in front of the Sashuis.

Now a choice

You can walk around the lake if you have time and energy. It's about half a kilometre and should take about ten minutes to do.

If that doesn't appeal, walk across the bridge in front of you to the other side of the lake. Once over turn left to walk through a little square with trees and a memorial to Flemish writer Maurets Sabbe.

Maurets Sabbe

It's unlikely you will have heard of any of his works, but perhaps the reason his statue was placed near the lock-house was because of one of his books was set here. It was titled, De filosoof van't sashuis, The Philosopher of the Lockhouse.

Pass the swans usually gathered on the left, cross the canal and pass an old nunnery building on the right – easy to spot with a statue of the Virgin Mary above one of the doors. Continue the walk from the horsehead fountain on page 74.

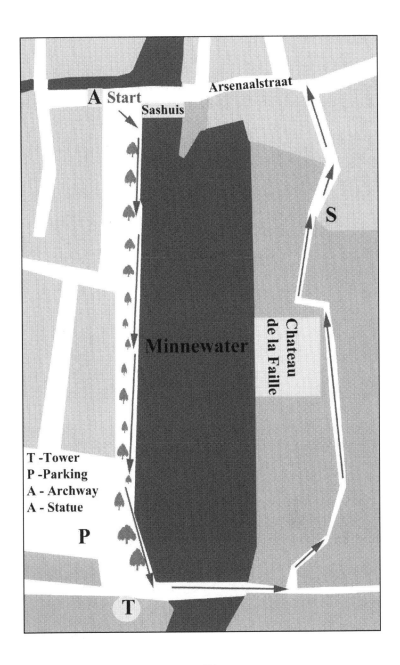

A Start
Sashuis
Arsenaalstraat

S

Minnewater

Chateau
de la Faille

T -Tower
P -Parking
A - Archway
A - Statue

P

T

Round Minnewater

If on the other hand you want to see the lake, you should stay on the Begijnhof side of the canal. Turn right to walk along the lakeside to the next bridge. As you do you will see the lovely Chateau de la Faille on the other side – it's now a restaurant.

The bridge at the top of the lake was crossed by hit-man Harry in the film "In Bruges", as it builds to its climax. Beside it stands the Poertoren.

This medieval tower is a remnant of Bruges's old city wall, and it was used to store gunpowder. There used to be a twin on the other side of the bridge.

Cross the bridge and once over turn left to walk through the park. You will reach some little houses. The first house has a statue of the Mary and Jesus on the side. Walk straight ahead along Minnewater with houses on either side.

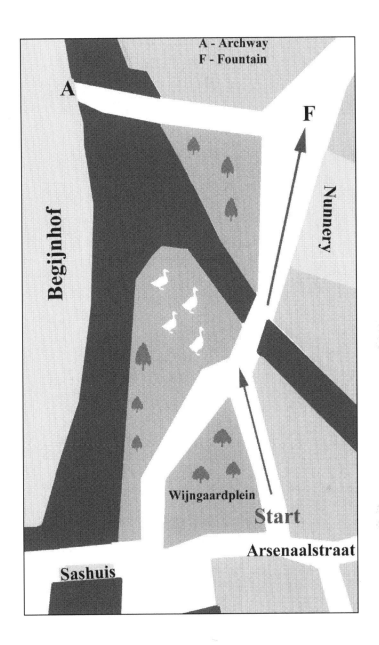

A - Archway
F - Fountain

Nunnery

Begijnhof

Wijngaardplein

Start

Arsenaalstraat

Sashuis

73

At the junction with Arsenaalstraat walk straight ahead into Wijngaardplein to re-cross the canal. You will pass an old nunnery building on the right – easy to spot with a statue of the Virgin Mary above one of the doors. You will reach the horsehead fountain again.

From the Horsehead Fountain

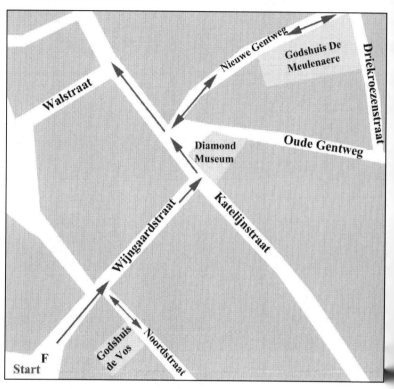

Stand next to the Horsehead fountain with the Begijnhof on your left, and walk into Wijngaardstraat. Turn right into Noordstraat to visit Godshuis de Vos.

Godshuis de Vos

Christiaan de Vos founded this godshuis in the early eighteenth century to house six poor widows. You can see the chapel where the widows prayed for their benefactor - it has the date1713 across the top, the year the complex was built. These days it still houses the elderly but the six houses have been converted into just four.

Backtrack to Wijngaardstraat and turn right. Continue straight ahead to the T junction with Katelijnestraat.

Turn left. There is a diamond museum on the right hand side of this street.

Diamond Museum

It's not included in the Brugge Museum card as it's privately owned but is free with the City Card. If you are interested in diamonds you might want to pop in to learn the history of diamonds and Belgium's involvement.

There is a demonstration of diamond polishing every day at 12:15; places are limited so if it appeals get there a bit beforehand.

Godshuis De Meulenaere

There is another alms-house nearby which is worth visiting, and it is only a few minutes' walk away. With the door of the Diamond Museum behind you, you will see there are two streets on your right, Oude Gentweg and Nieuwe Gentweg. Go down Nieuwe Gentweg and you will pass the whitewashed wall of Godshuis De Meulenaere. The green door which gives you access stands at the far end – there is a statue of the Virgin Mary above it.

It is one of the largest almshouses and many think it's the best. It has a lovely green garden and you can escape from the tourist trail for a few minutes.

When you are ready to continue, backtrack along Nieuwe Gotweg and turn right into Katelijnstraat once more. Pass Walstraat on your left.

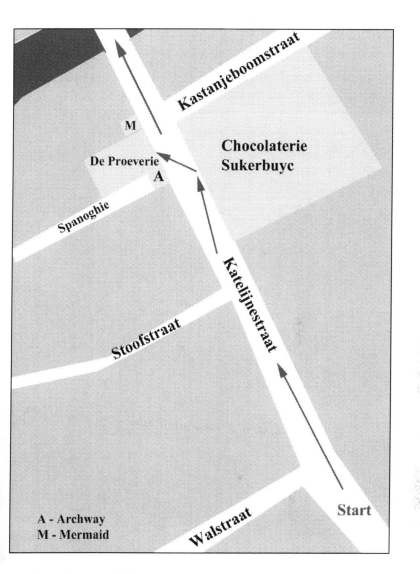

Kastanjeboomstraat

M

De Proeverie

A

Chocolaterie
Sukerbuyc

Spanoghie

Katelijnestraat

Stoofstraat

Start

A - Archway
M - Mermaid

Walstraat

Chocolaterie Sukerbuyc

Continue along Katelijnstraat until you reach the Godshuis
Spanoghe again, you will see the oldest chocolate shop in

Bruges on your right. You can see right into the kitchen where the chocolates are being made from the shop window.

Opposite on the other side of the street there is a nice tearoom, called De Proeverie. You could have a coffee or even better, a hot chocolate – the chocolate comes from Chocolaterie Sukerbuyc across the road.

With the door of De Proeverie behind you, turn left along Katelijnstraat to reach the canal.

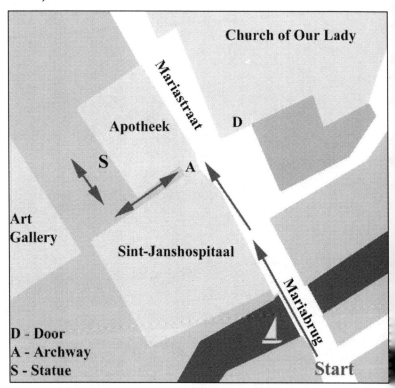

Cross the canal to walk back down Mariastraat. On your left you will come to what looks like a church but is actually St John's hospital. You passed it earlier on the walk.

St. Johns hospital

St John's hospital was founded in the 12th century and was staffed both by religious and lay doctors and nurses. They cared for the poor, the needy, the elderly and the homeless. It was a hospital until 1976!

On top of the entrance you can see Saint John in pilgrim garb. It's a huge building and it houses many interesting artefacts so have a walk around.

There is a large painting showing the hospital when it was full of beds and patients, with the nuns and doctors doing their best to help the afflicted. Remember that in medieval times, medicine was in its infancy and hospitals were places to be dreaded. If you went into one, you very often did not come out again, at least not vertically. Many of the patients who didn't make it are buried under your feet.

Hans Memling was a German born artist who settled in Bruges and he was a patient at one time in the hospital. There are several of his paintings on show and you will eventually reach the museum inside the hospital. The most famous items are "The Mystic Marriage of St. Catherine" and the "Shrine of St. Ursula".

Saint Ursula

Saint Ursula's legend is probably a bit more fanciful than most. She decided to travel from Britain to Rome in the company of 11,000 virgin handmaidens. This was at a time when the choice was, walk or ride a horse, so already the logistics are incredible. They had the bad luck to run into a tribe of Huns in Germany, and Ursula was given the choice of marrying the chieftain or dying along with the eleven thousand virgins. She refused to marry and they were all slaughtered. It seems an odd reason to be made a saint.

If you look in the six windows of the shrine you will see depictions of her story. One of the paintings also shows two nuns kneeling before Mary – they are Jacosa van Dudzeele and Anna van den Moortele who actually commissioned the shrine for the hospital.

The Mystic Marriage of Saint Catherine

The Mystic Marriage of Saint Catherine is the centre panel of the St John Altarpiece which was commissioned for the hospital. She is the princess wearing a crown and reaching towards baby Jesus. She is sitting to the left of the Virgin Mary

Saint Catherine of Alexandria was a princess from the fourth century. She became a Christian and devoted herself to her religion and to Jesus. Emperor Maximian had her whipped and imprisoned to make her give up her religion. When that failed he condemned her to die on a breaking wheel – she was to be tied to a wooden wheel and bludgeoned to death. However, when Catherine touched the wheel it shattered. Maximian gave up on the torture at that point and had her beheaded instead. If you have watched Catherine Wheels spin round at a fireworks show, they represent the breaking wheel which failed to kill Saint Catharine.

In the painting you can see Catherine is kneeling on the wheel, and baby Jesus is placing a ring on her finger - that's the mystic marriage.

Once you are back outside turn left to find the archway into St John's hospital courtyard.

St John's hospital Courtyard

On the right hand side of the courtyard is the old Apothecary of the hospital, which is also a museum and worth a look if you have the Bruges Museum card. Note however that it shuts at lunchtime, and has a very long lunch hour!

It was built in the seventeenth century and was still in use until 1971. If you visit you can gaze at the original furnishings, and pharmacist's jars, pots, and bottles. Spot the huge mortar where herbal ingredients were pulverised to turn them into medicines.

On the other side of the courtyard is the museum of modern art. It doesn't hold any major well known works, but lots of sketches by all the famous artists. It doesn't too take long to walk round and you might giggle at some of the Picasso sketches.

Once you return to Mariastraat you are facing the Church of Our Lady where this walk ends.

If you want to reconnect with Walk 1, turn left to reach a junction and take the middle road, Heilige-Geeststraat. Resume Walk 1 from Heillige Geeststraat on page 49.

Walk 3 – Bruges North

Walk 3 also begins in Markt. It will take you into a much quieter part of Bruges before reaching one of its most beautiful squares.

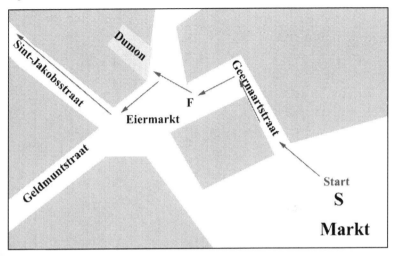

Stand back-to-back with the statue of Coninck and Breydel. Directly ahead of you is little Geernaartstraat which is full of restaurants. It bends to the left and ends in the Eiermarkt, a little square with a fountain topped with the lion of Flanders and the bear of Bruges.

Across the road you will see a very old building housing Dumon.

Dumon

This is a very good chocolatier so you might want to buy some souvenirs or just take note of its location for later. It's a family business, headed by Madame Dumon. Don't be afraid to ask for help in choosing your chocs.

Face the front of Dumon and turn left. Take the first right into Sint-Jakobsstraat.

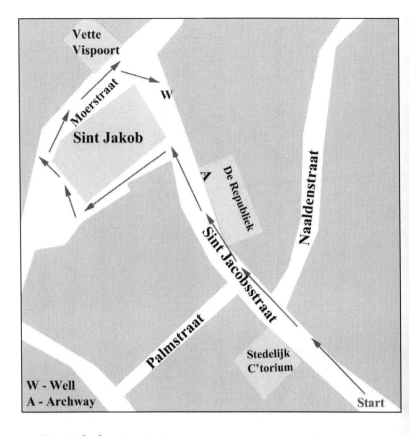

Vette Vispoort

Moerstraat

W

Sint Jakob

De Republiek

Naaldenstraat

A

Sint Jacobsstraat

Palmstraat

Stedelijk C'torium

W - Well
A - Archway

Start

Sint-Jakobsstraat

You are now entering a much less touristy part of Bruges, but just as lovely as the better known parts with stepped gabled houses lining the streets. Pass the Stedelijk Conservatorium with its impressive wooden door on your left. Also pass Naaldenstraat on your right.

Sint Jakobsstraat will bend right, and as it does you will reach the De Republiek building on the right. It's easy to spot because it's proclaimed across the top. At the far end of the building is an archway which gives access to the Lumiere cinema and a courtyard with some shops and cafes.

Lumiere cinema

Cinema Lumière has three small viewing rooms at the moment with plans to expand to four. The screens are called The Blue Room, The Red Room, and the Green Room – yes they are decorated in those colours. Its aim is to be a theatre for everyone and it shows a wide range of films, especially foreign films with subtitles, which means that you have a good chance of catching a film in English!

Continue along Sint Jakobsstraat. You will see the steeple of the Sint Jakob church ahead of you. As you reach the church you will find a little brick archway on your left which will take you to the front of the church.

Sint Jakob Church

This area was built and populated by the well-to-do of Bruges in the thirteenth century. They replaced the small church which once stood here with this much grander affair.

If it's open go inside to see the bright and cheerful interior with its astonishingly intricate carved pulpit – the theme is the spread of Christianity around the world, so there are characters from America, Europe, Africa and India.

You will also see a multitude of paintings. At one time it had even more by famous Flemish artists, placed in private altars by the wealthy community. However the iconoclasm which destroyed so many beautiful things in the sixteenth century hit this church as well. Some of the better known works survived but are now in the Groeninge Museum which you have probably already visited.

Ferry do Gros chapel

Find the Ferry do Gros chapel which is thought to be the prettiest in Bruges. It was commissioned by Ferry de Gros who was treasurer of The Order of the Golden Fleece and very rich. At the top is Ferry himself next to his first wife. Beneath them is the tomb of his second wife.

Saint Lucy

Also worth spotting is the three panelled painting showing part of the legend of Saint Lucy from Sicily. She had a vision of Saint Agatha, and consequently decided to devote her life to God. Unfortunately her mother had already organised her wedding but the first panel shows her agreeing to cancel it. The second panel shows the furious bride-groom denouncing Lucy to the Romans for being a Christian. The Roman governor condemned her to a life of prostitution, but when the guards came to take her away they could not move her. The third panel shows them tying her to some oxen but even they could not budge her.

The story actually goes on but is not illustrated by the artists. The guards then tore her eyes out but God put them back, they set her on fire but God put it out. Finally they stabbed her and she died – perhaps God was doing something else at that point.

No-one knows who the artist was so he has been given the name:

Master of the Legend of Saint Lucy

When you exit, face the church door and go round the left-hand side into Moerstraat. Watch for an opening on your left just after number 18. It doesn't look very inviting but it will take you into Vette Vispoort.

Vette Vispoort

Vette Vispoort has several single-storey whitewashed houses which were built in the sixteenth century, each one is a godshuis. A godshuis was generally built by the wealthy to house a poor family. The lucky family's only obligation was to pray for their benefactors, which must have seemed a very good deal to the homeless.

Return to Moerstraat and turn left. Just past the church you will reach a little square with an old well on the right.

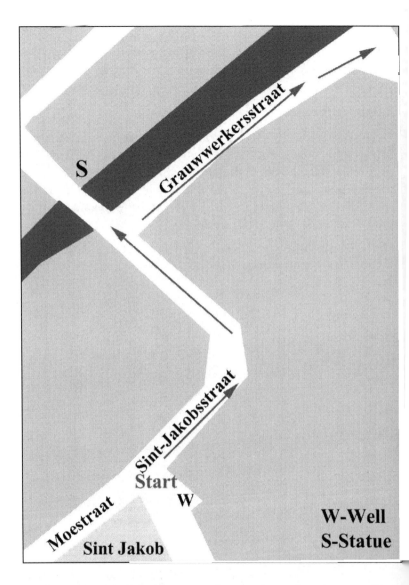

Continue walking away from the church on Sint-Jakobsstraat as it swings left. You will reach a bridge over a lovely canal with tiny gardens lining the canal-sides. Don't cross it, but do spot the lovely little statue of Mary and Jesus on the corner of one of the buildings at the bridge. Turn right along Grauwwerkersstraat to enjoy walking along the canalside.

Grauwwerkersstraat translates as Grey Worker Street, but it doesn't mean that the people who worked here were all elderly. This was where Bruges's fur trade was centred and the name comes from the colour of the Russian squirrel pelts they worked with.

If you visited the Groeninge Museum on Walk 1 you might have spotted the painting of Margaret Van Eyck, wearing a gown with what is thought to be a squirrel collar.

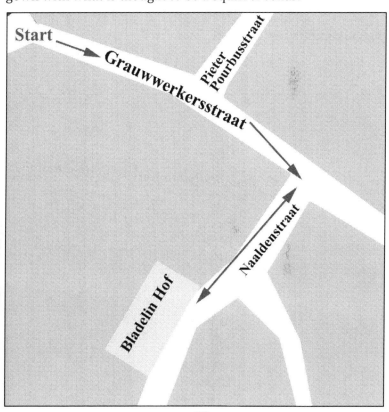

Grauwwerkersstraat will swing right so follow it past Pieter Pourbusstraat on your left. Turn right down Naaldenstraat to reach the huge Bladelin Court on your right.

Bladelin Court

This castle like building was commissioned by Pieter Bladelin in the fourteenth century. He was treasurer of the Order of the Golden Fleece so clearly very powerful.

If you visit you will see the pretty inner court. Take a look at the stone medallion decorating it – they show Lorenzo de Medici – he was one of the most powerful rulers of Florence. When the Medici family decided they needed to expand their banking empire to Bruges, they chose this building. Its situation was ideal for banking as it was next to Bruges's financial centre which you will see shortly.

Return along Naaldenstraat to Grauwwerkersstraat.

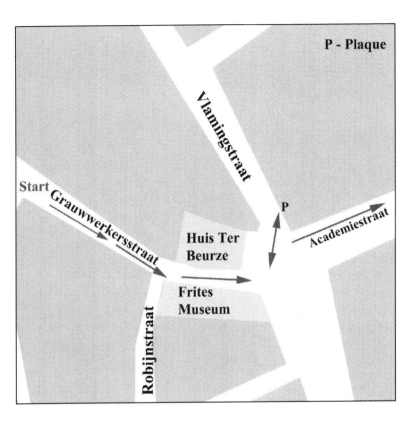

Turn right and pass little Robijnstraat on your right. You will soon reach busy Vlamingstraat. Immediately on your right is the Frites Museum.

Frites Museum

This is a private museum which tells the story of the potato and frites, which are said to have been invented in Belgium. It is probably of limited interest to most people, but if you are keen on potatoes and their friability you could visit.

Before you leave take a look at the building itself - it was the headquarters of the Genoese merchants. If you look up to the arch above the entrance you can see St George dispatching the dragon – St George is the patron saint of Genoa.

On the other side of Grauwwerkersstraat stands the Huis Ter Beurze

Huis Ter Beurze

This was the home of the Van der Beurze family.

Bruges was a hub of financial dealing between the German and the Mediterranean merchants and traders. The role of intermediary between the traders fell to the well-respected innkeepers of Bruges, and the Beurze family was one of the most important.

Their inn was called the 'Ter Buerze inn and the square it sat on became the financial centre of Bruges. It was where deals were made and vital trade information was exchanged. By the fourteenth century it was where currency and bonds were traded under strict rules, using rates from the banking centres of Europe. The Van der Beurze family home is said to be the world's first stock exchange building.

The word Beurze spread over Europe and was adopted by many languages as more cities built their own Stock Exchanges. It was even used in London until the eighteenth century, when it was renamed the "Royal Exchange".

When you are ready to continue, stand with the Frites Museum door behind you. You will see Vlamingstraat to your left and right, and Academiestraat in front of you. Take a few steps left into Vlamingstraat and find a plaque on your right hand side of the street.

Dante

Dante of course wrote the famous "Divine Comedy", and in one of its many verses it discusses the Bruges-Wissamnt dike. So Bruges has erected this plaque to commemorate its mention in such a memorable piece of literature.

As the Flemings, living with the constant threat
of flood tides rushing in between Wissant
and Bruges, build their dikes to force the sea back

Return to stand with the Frites Museum door behind you.
This time walk straight ahead into Academiestraat.

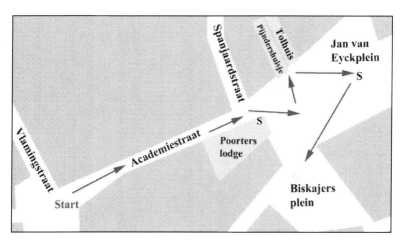

As you approach Jan van Eyck Plein you will walk along the
side of the Poorterslodge on your right.

The north side of Bruges was where ships used to arrive to
unload their many goods for market. So it was here that
administrative buildings were built to legislate and gather
import taxes. The Poorterslodge was built in the fourteenth
century and was where the most important traders and
merchants met their trading partners. These days it
safeguards the state archives.

Poorterslodge

When you reach the corner of the Poorterslodge, spot the
little statue of a bear – he represents the Society of the White
Bear, an ancient organisation which arranged tournaments in

Bruges where knights could knock each other off their horses. Their headquarters was in the Poorterslodge.

Continue into Jan van Eyck Plein to reach the front of the building to see it at its best. It caught fire in 1755 but was restored.

Now face the Poorterslodge and turn right to see two extremely narrow buildings with red doors.

Tolhuis

The one with the colourful coat of arms is the Tolhuis. The coat of arms belonged to Pieter van Luxemburg who was also a knight of the Order of the Golden Fleece. He was given the right to levy a toll on any goods brought into Bruges over the bridge which once stood here – truly money for doing nothing!

Pijndershuisje

The narrow building just to the left of the Tolhuis is the Pijndershuisje – which means the House of the Stevedores (dockworkers). It commemorates the hard-working men who kept the goods flowing in and out of Bruges with some tiny little statues holding the building up – they are hunched just above the door and beneath the much larger 4 statues.

Now walk into the middle of the square. From here you get the best view of the Poorterslodge with its narrow tower.

Jan Van Eyck

In the middle of the square stands Van Eyck himself. You can get a lovely snap of Van Eyck with the canal behind him.

Van Eyck is one of the best known Flemish painters. He moved into Bruges once he had found fame and fortune and made it his home. If you visited the Groeninge Museum on Walk 1 you will have seen some of his works. If you have seen the movie "Monuments Men", you will have heard of the "Ghent Altarpiece". It was one of the masterpieces which had been stolen by the Nazis and which the Monuments Men were trying to recover. It was painted by Jan and his brother Hubert, and is a must-see if you ever visit Ghent

This is a nice spot for refreshments if needed. When you are ready to move on face the Poorterslodge and turn left to exit via a shady little square called Biskajersplein.

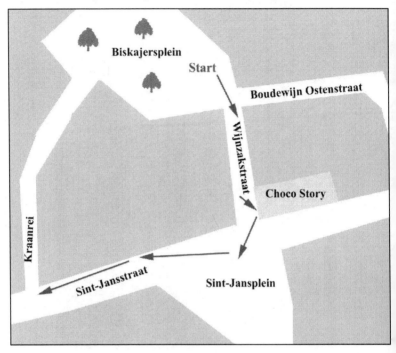

Keep to the left of the square and walk into Wijnzakstraat. At the end of Wijnzakstraat you will reach Sint-Jansplein

Sint-Jansplein

This old square got its name from an old church which once stood here but didn't survive the centuries. The square was also a marketplace. These days it's quiet except for visitors to Choco Story which is on the corner of Wijnzakstraat.

It's another private museum, this time telling the history of chocolate from the trees in South America to the chocolate

96

makers in Belgium. Again it's probably of limited interest to most people, but if you are intrigued you could visit.

From Wijnzakstraat with Choco story on your left, turn right to walk along the side of the square into Sint-Jansstraat.

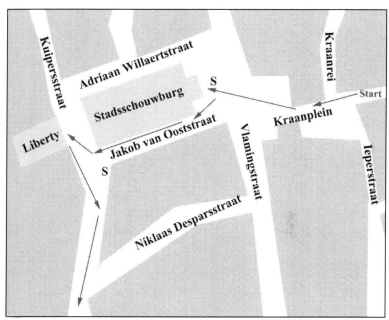

Walk straight ahead through Kraanplein, passing Kraanrei on your right. You will return to wide Vlamingstraat once more. Cross Vlamingstraat diagonally right to reach Stadsschouwburg.

Stadsschouwburg

This is an old theatre built in 1865. It has an ornate interior with a wonderful chandelier which was constructed in Berlin. There are guided tours every day, so you could enquire at the theatre if you are interested.

Papageno

Papageno stands in front of the theatre. He appears in Mozart's 'The Magic Flute' and is a bird catcher who uses panpipes to charm the birds. You can see he is wearing a hat shaped like a bird, holding his pipes in his right hand, and has already caught 3 birds which are in his cage. It's a relatively new statue, only put up in 1980.

Face Papageno and walk around the left-hand side of the theatre to reach Kuipersstraat. Here you will find another statue, this time of three size zero ladies. They are by Joseph de Loose from Bruges.

Liberty Cinema

Just opposite the back of the theatre is another of Bruges's old cinemas, The Liberty. At the time of writing this one is still going strong so have a look at what's on.

Face the cinema and turn left along Kuipersstraat passing Niklaas Desparsstraat on your left.

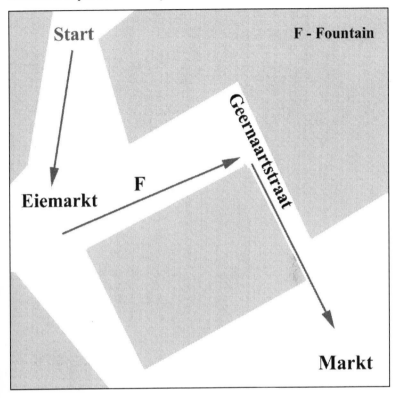

You will reach the Eiemarkt and its fountain once more. You will see the belfry peeping over the buildings, so turn left at the fountain and follow Geernaartstraat to return to Markt.

A Reward

If you feel like a beer, there is another very nice bar worth visiting with an interesting legend – Cambrinus.

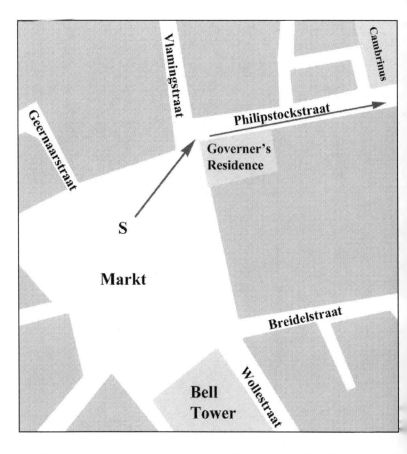

If that idea appeals to you, stand back-to-back with Coninck and Breydel and cross the square diagonally right to reach the corner of the Governor's Residence. Turn right into Philipstockstraat – and the bar is three blocks along on the left.

Cambrinus

The building dates from the start of the eighteenth century. At the top you can see depictions of the Devil, the Sun, and the Moon. Below them are gods and goddesses said to represent the seasons. Venus represents Spring, Ceres represents

Summer, Bacchus represents Autumn, and Diana represents Winter.

Cambrinus was a legendary king who is said to have invented beer. You can see a statue of the king himself at the corner of the building holding a foaming mug of beer aloft. Walk around the corner and you will see him again, engraved on the window glass, this time accompanied by a lady and again raising a mug of beer. So why not pop in and follow his example.

Did you enjoy these walks?

I do hope you found these walks both fun and interesting, and I would love feedback. If you have any comments, either good or bad, please review this book

Other Belgian Gems

Why not visit Ghent or Antwerp while you are in Belgium. They are both just a train ride away from Bruges and full of interesting sights:

Strolling Around Ghent

Strolling Around Antwerp

Made in the USA
San Bernardino, CA
21 April 2018